Healthy Eating

NB

Fruits

Nancy Dickmann

www.raintreepublishers.co.uk
Visit our website to find out
more information about
Raintree books.

To order:

☎ Phone 0845 6044371

▤ Fax +44 (0) 1865 312263

▧ Email myorders@raintreepublishers.co.uk

Customers from outside the UK please telephone +44 1865 312262

Raintree is an imprint of Capstone Global Library Limited, a company incorporated in England and Wales having its registered office at 7 Pilgrim Street, London, EC4V 6LB – Registered company number: 6695582

Text © Capstone Global Library Limited 2010
First published in hardback in 2010
Paperback edition first published in 2011
The moral rights of the proprietor have been asserted.

Edited by Sian Smith, Nancy Dickmann, and Rebecca Rissman
Designed by Joanna Hinton-Malivoire
Picture research by Elizabeth Alexander
Production by Victoria Fitzgerald
Originated by Capstone Global Library Ltd
Printed and bound in China by South China Printing Company Ltd

ISBN 978 0 431 00399 3 (hardback)
14 13 12 11 10
10 9 8 7 6 5 4 3 2 1

ISBN 978 0 431 00960 5 (paperback)
15 14 13 12 11
10 9 8 7 6 5 4 3 2 1

British Library Cataloguing in Publication Data
Dickmann, Nancy.
    Fruits. -- (Healthy eating)
    1. Fruit--Juvenile literature. 2. Fruit in human
    nutrition--Juvenile literature.
    I. Title II. Series
    641.3'4-dc22

Acknowledgements
We would like to thank the following for permission to reproduce photographs: © Capstone Publishers p.**22** (Karon Dubke); Alamy p.**11** (© Bloom Works Inc.); Food Standards Agency/ © Crown copyright material is reproduced with the permission of the Controller of HMSO and Queen's Printer for Scotland p.**19**; Getty Images pp.**8** (Rosemary Calvert/Photographer's Choice), **17** (Alistair Berg/Digital Vision), **20**, **23 middle** (Heinrich van den Berg/Gallo Images); iStockphoto pp.**5**, **7** (© Elena Korenbaum), **13** (© Suprijono Suharjoto), **23 top** (© Mark Hatfield); Photolibrary pp. **9**, **13** (John Smith/Fancy), **10** (Pixtal Images), **14** (Medicimage), **15** (PureStock), **16** (Radius Images), **21** (Willy De L'Horme/Photononstop); Shutterstock pp.**4** (© Denis and Yulia Pogostins), **6** (© Georgios Alexandris), **12** (© Simone van den Berg), **18** (© Monkey Business Images).

Front cover photograph of fruit reproduced with permission of © Capstone Publishers (Karon Dubke). Back cover photograph reproduced with permission of iStockphoto (© Suprijono Suharjoto).

We would like to thank Dr Sarah Schenker for her invaluable help in the preparation of this book.

Every effort has been made to contact copyright holders of material reproduced in this book. Any omissions will be rectified in subsequent printings if notice is given to the publishers.

Contents

What are fruits?

Fruits are parts of plants.

Eating fruits can keep us healthy.

orange

Some fruits grow on trees.

vine

grapes

Some fruits grow on vines.

Looking at fruits

orange

Many fruits are round.

Fruits can be many different colours.

grapes

raisins

We dry some fruits. Raisins are dried grapes.

We make juice from some fruits.

How fruits help us

Fruits are full of nutrients.

You need nutrients to stay healthy.

Eating bananas keeps your blood healthy.

Eating kiwis helps you fight colds.

Eating fruits helps your body
make energy.

You need energy to work
and play.

Healthy eating

We need to eat five servings of fruit and vegetables each day.

fruit and vegetables

The eatwell plate shows us which foods to eat.

Staying healthy

We eat fruits to stay healthy.

We eat fruits because they taste good!

Find the fruit

Here is a healthy breakfast.

Can you find the fruits?

Answer on page 24

Picture glossary

blood red liquid inside your body. Blood takes food and air to all your body parts.

energy the power to do something. We need energy when we work or play.

nutrients things our bodies need to stay healthy. You can get nutrients in different foods.

Index

Answer to quiz on page 22: The fruits are strawberries in the bowl, and oranges which have been made into orange juice in the glass.

Notes for parents and teachers

Before reading

Explain that we need to eat a range of different foods to stay healthy. Splitting foods into different groups can help us understand how much food we should eat from each group. Introduce the fruit and vegetables group. How many different fruits can the children think of? Explain that eating at least five portions of fruits and vegetables every day can help us to stay healthy.

After reading

• Play "Guess the mystery fruit". Place a fruit or fruit picture into a bag. Alternatively, choose a fruit from the cover of this book. Give the children clues to help them identify the fruit. For example, "It has pips. It tastes sour. It grows on a tree." Take turns to describe different fruits.

• Ask the children to bring in some fruits. These could be their favourite fruits or fruits they have never tried before. Share the fruits with the class. Explain that our taste buds change and why it is good to try new things. Create a pictogram to show the class's favourite fruits.

• Ask the children to sit in a circle with one child standing in the centre. Choose four different fruits and give one fruit name to each child. When the child in the centre calls out a fruit, everyone with that fruit name should swap places. The child in the centre should try to find a place to sit. The caller can also choose to call out "fruit salad". If they do so, everyone in the circle needs to swap places.